· Greenwich and the Thames ·

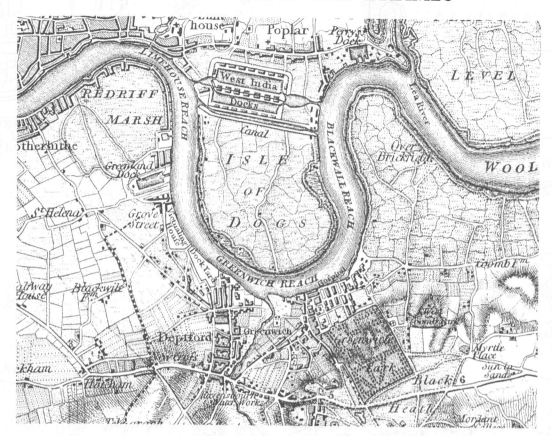

reenwich lies at the eastern approach to London, where the Thames sags before winding its way towards the city. Historically, anyone attacking London from Europe via Dover was forced either over Blackheath by land or past Greenwich by river.

Defence, celebration or service of the city and its river have always been key to the prosperity of the borough, which includes Blackheath, Charlton, Deptford, Eltham, Plumstead and Woolwich, together with Greenwich itself.

Each is close enough to central London to feed off the wealth of the city, while far enough away to have its own particular characteristics.

There was a time when the Thames was crowded with shipping and cargo from all over the world, making the riverbanks temporarily the most prosperous on earth.

Occasionally the mud of the area throws up some shard of London's hidden past. The construction site digging which is part of Greenwich's brave new future has revealed some clues about the area's ancient inhabitants. As yet there is no proof that anyone lived along this once marshy stretch of the Thames before the Romans came to Britain; probably they did not live here either. Roman relics dug up in Greenwich in 1902 are thought to have come from an isolated temple, stranded on the way to Londinium proper, which the Romans had established upriver by AD43.

By the 2nd century AD, flat-bottomed barges were regularly lugging loads into Londinium as a low-key sign of the traffic to come. The next invaders were the Saxons, in the 6th century. The first real proof that any of them settled in Greenwich comes in the 10th century, when it is recorded that the Saxon King Edgar gave part of his property in the area to the Abbey of Ghent. The hugely complicated saga of the

LEFT
*Nicholas Hawksmoor
built St Alfege's in 1714
on the site of earlier
churches marking the spot
where Alfege, Archbishop
of Canterbury,
had been murdered.*

ABOVE
*A view from the air of
Greenwich, a World
Heritage Site, with the
Royal Naval College to
the left and the royal park
stretching southwards
towards Blackheath.*

ownership and development of this ancient property, which is partly defined today by the royal park, meanders through the story of Greenwich much as the river on which it stands bends and curves.

After the Saxons came the Danes, and successive Scandinavian raids which peaked tragically during an 11th-century invasion. Longboats were moored at Greenwich on and off for four years. In 1011 the Danes kidnapped Archbishop Alfege from Canterbury. But when their ransom bid went wrong they murdered him – where Hawksmoor's Church of St Alfege now stands in the centre of Greenwich.

· A NAVAL PRESENCE ·

By the 16th century much naval ship-building was taking place along the banks of the Thames, with royal dock-yards at Deptford and downriver at Woolwich. In 1514 Henry VIII launched his flagship, the *Henri Grace à Dieu*, at Woolwich. She was the largest ship in the largest navy England had ever seen. The powerful naval presence meant that no foreign vessel, Danish or otherwise, would ever attack London again. This stretch of the Thames continued to produce most of Britain's warships until 1869.

The days of England's naval supremacy had their ceremonial peak in 1806 with the funeral of her most famous admiral, Lord Nelson, after his defeat of the French at Trafalgar. On Christmas Day 1805 his body was carried ashore at Greenwich Hospital – now the Royal Naval College – in readiness for the three-day lying-in-state in the Painted Hall on 5 January.

Tens of thousands of people clogged Greenwich for days, desperate to pay their respects. And then all shipping was cleared from the river to allow the fabulous flotilla of gilt barges with ceremonial flags to accompany the body upstream to St Paul's Cathedral for the funeral and burial in the crypt.

Turner's famous painting *The Fighting Téméraire*, sketched near Greenwich in 1838, shows a different type of funeral. Steam belches into the sky from a little iron tug as it tows the ghostly old wooden man-of-war to the breaker's yard. By this time wood and sail were giving way to iron and steam, forcing ship-building increasingly to the North where the raw materials were. The naval yards at Woolwich and Deptford closed in 1869. The last Thames-built Royal Navy ship, HMS *Thunderer*, was launched across the river from Greenwich at Bow Creek in 1912.

LEFT
Sir Peter Lely's portrait of
Peter Pett, the master
shipwright at the Royal
Dockyard, Woolwich,
where the famous vessel
Sovereign of the Seas
was constructed in 1637.
Pepys, the diarist,
described the ship as 'a
glorious vessel … being
for defence and ornament
the richest that ever spread
cloth before the wind'.

BELOW LEFT
William Parrott's 1841
view of the Dreadnought,
a hospital ship moored
upstream from Greenwich
Hospital. Merchant and
disabled seamen of any
nationality were main-
tained and clothed on the
massive hulk.

LEFT
L.F. Abbott's
portrait of
Nelson in 1798-9
after the battle
of the Nile.

· THE PALACE SAGA ·

The historic heart of Greenwich comprises the park, the old Royal Observatory perched on its hill and the view down to the river from there, taking in the Queen's House, the National Maritime Museum and the Royal Naval College. This area roughly corresponds to the estate that the Saxons had made over to the Abbey of Ghent in the 10th century.

By 1433 the land was in Crown hands again and the austere abbey on the site of the present Royal Naval College had become the worldly Bella Court, home to Henry V's brother, Humphrey, Duke of Gloucester. The Duke also built a fortress on the hill, where the Royal Observatory now stands, in his newly enclosed park.

After the Duke died in 1447, Bella Court was given to his nephew Henry VI's teenage wife, Margaret of Anjou. In spite of the changes she made to it (which included re-naming the house Placentia), the place seems to have all but vanished by 1500, the year that Henry VII bought 600,000 bricks and created the spectacular Greenwich Palace, an enormous castellated residence that dominated the river for 160 years.

Henry VIII was born here and grew to love the place, especially for elaborate

ABOVE
Greenwich Palace from the river, from an early 17th-century painting.

LEFT
Elizabeth I at the time of the threatened Spanish invasion. In August 1588 she travelled from Green-wich to Tilbury to review her Armada troops and make her famous rallying speech.

ABOVE RIGHT
*Johannes Vorsterman's
1676 view of Greenwich
shows the Tudor palace in
ruins and the Queen's
House enjoying an unin-
terrupted view of the
Thames for the first time.
The west wing of Charles
II's abandoned 'King's
House' was later rescued
and became part of the
Royal Naval College.*

parties, hunting and gallant jousting tourna-
ments. This gallantry however did not prevent
him replacing his wife, Catherine of Aragon,
with Anne Boleyn, whose daughter, Elizabeth I,
was also born here.

Elizabeth loved Greenwich Palace, from
where she could gaze at the river, watching the
world go by – or at least watching explorers go
by – on their way to find out what the world
looked like. Martin Frobisher sailed past here
to look for the North West Passage, and it was
on the *Golden Hind* by Greenwich that Queen
Elizabeth watched Sir Francis Drake being
knighted after he had circumnavigated the
globe. Greenwich may also have been the
place where Sir Walter Raleigh famously laid
his cloak down over a puddle for the Virgin
Queen to walk on.

BELOW
*Charles II intended to
replace Greenwich Palace
but work stopped in 1665.
Queen Mary II asked
Wren to complete the
buildings as a hospital for
veteran sailors, insisting
that the grand vista from
the Queen's House to the
river should not be
impeded. The Royal
Naval College's 125-year
occupancy began in 1873.*

· THE QUEEN'S HOUSE ·

One of Greenwich's headiest eras ended in 1603 with the death of Queen Elizabeth, and the royal estate was largely neglected until James I gave it to his queen, Anne of Denmark. It was for her that Inigo Jones began to build the architecturally radical Queen's House – although she died in 1619 before it was finished.

By the time the Queen's House was nearing completion in 1635, Charles I was on the throne, but his wife, Henrietta Maria, was unable to enjoy the house before the Civil War drove her to France. During Cromwell's Commonwealth, the Queen's House fared better than the palace, which was turned first into a barracks and then later a biscuit factory.

Charles II returned from France after the restoration of the monarchy with plans to rebuild Greenwich Palace. But the Great Plague put paid to his scheme. He lost interest and his new 'King's House', only partly finished, languished until it was incorporated into the Greenwich Hospital.

But Charles did at least realise one new and far-reaching dream – an observatory on the hill, and Henrietta Maria, now the Queen Mother, returned briefly to live in the Queen's House before her death in France in 1669.

LEFT
Henrietta Maria by Van Dyck. Before she went into exile in 1644 she had ordered furnishings and paintings for her 'house of delight', which she enjoyed after her return in 1660.

BELOW
Doors leading to the black-and-white marble loggia from where the visitor to the Queen's House can take in a splendid view of the park and the old Royal Observatory on the hill.

RIGHT
The open-well 'Tulip' staircase, the first of its kind in England. The spiralling stone steps lead to a skylight in the roof.

OPPOSITE LEFT
The Great Hall, a perfect cube, has a marble floor and an intricately carved wooden balustrade. The ceiling is a copy of the Gentileschi original removed to Marlborough House in London in the 18th century.

INSET RIGHT
Inigo Jones, the designer of the Queen's House. William Hogarth's portrait was modelled on a drawing by Van Dyck.

THE QUEEN'S HOUSE
The Queen's House, the first Classical domestic house in England, was inspired by the Italian villas of Andrea Palladio. It is now part of the National Maritime Museum.

• GREENWICH HOSPITAL & ROYAL NAVAL COLLEGE •

The new palace began to decay and might have disappeared altogether after William and Mary came to the throne in 1689 had it not been for another royal enthusiasm: the idea of building a hospital for veteran sailors. Queen Mary made this the 'darling object of her life', but died of smallpox in 1694 before seeing it realised. Sir Christopher Wren, supported by Sir John Vanbrugh and Nicholas Hawksmoor, turned her dream into London's greatest example of the grand English Baroque style.

But not without problems. Wren's original plan for Greenwich Hospital hid the Queen's House. Mary complained, forcing Wren to slice his design in two, cleaving the façade to create an uninterrupted view from the river to the comparatively tiny building which was at the time being used as the home of the Ranger of Greenwich Park.

The 42 disabled men who limped into the colossus when it opened in 1705 must have felt distinctly overshadowed. Numbers slowly increased to a total of 3,000. But by 1850 most

LEFT
Wren's chapel was rebuilt by James 'Athenian' Stuart after a fire in 1779. The altar painting is by Benjamin West.

LEFT
James Thornhill took 19 years to paint allegorical scenes on the ceilings and walls of the magnificent Painted Hall.

of the sailors of Nelson's era were dead, and progressively fewer veterans needed or wanted the spartan conditions hidden behind the opulent façades. The hospital closed in 1869, the same year as the Woolwich Dockyards.

In 1873 the Royal Naval College took over the buildings; the chapel and magnificent Painted Hall were opened to the public. The Royal Navy remained until 1998 but the educational function of the college continues into the new Millennium as students of the University of Greenwich and of the Trinity College of Music will occupy the buildings.

RIGHT
Sir Christopher Wren, a 1711 portrait by Sir Godfrey Kneller.

BELOW
Dr Johnson considered Greenwich Hospital 'far too magnificent for a place of charity'. Soon after the last elderly sailors departed in 1869, the buildings became the Royal Naval College.

· THE NATIONAL MARITIME MUSEUM ·

The National Maritime Museum was founded in 1934. It is a spectacular cele-bration of Britain, Greenwich and the sea. The old Royal Observatory and the Queen's House, two of the finest buildings in the country, are part of the museum, but the real focus for the enormous maritime collection (there are over two million items in all) is the complex of galleries joined by a colonnade to the Queen's House. This west wing, and a simi-lar one to the east of the house, were built after the Queen's House became a school for the children of seamen in 1806.

The Nelson gallery not only covers the exploits of Britain's greatest naval hero, but also gives a fascinating insight into the consuming national interest that followed the admiral's death at the moment of his greatest triumph. Objects from Nelson's extraordinary life almost took on the significance of reli-gious relics. One such is the uniform coat that he wore when he died, which is laid out here for all to see. In the 20th-century Sea Power gallery paintings, photographs, models and interactive displays shed

dramatic light on war at sea from the beginning of the century until the present day.

In the last years of the 20th century, £20 million have been spent redeveloping the galleries to include 16 new ones, housed in and around a great courtyard covered by a huge glazed roof. Exhibits in the refurbished museum include sumptuous royal barges resembling the one used to take Nelson's body from Greenwich to St Paul's for burial and displays covering everything from navigation to exploration. There is also an interactive All Hands gallery aimed at bringing maritime history to life for children.

FAR LEFT
The ornately decorated state barge of Frederick, Prince of Wales, eldest son of George II. It is one of several elaborate barges in the museum.

CENTRE
One of the giant anchors outside the museum. The west wing has been extensively rebuilt to enable many artefacts in the reserve collections to be shown.

· PIVOT OF THE WORLD ·

Greenwich stands on the prime meridian, the imaginary line running between the North and South poles, from which all other longitudinal lines spread east and west to divide the globe into measurable segments over which the sun passes at regular intervals. The use of Greenwich for this purpose derives from Charles II's shrewd decision to build an observatory here in 1675. Again, the impetus came from the river and the sea.

Ships that left London to conquer or trade abroad needed better navigation; mapping out longitude was a way to achieve this. Charles was advised that this would best be done by observing the moon and the stars over a long period. So Christopher Wren designed an observatory which would not merely be efficient but would have appropriate 'pompe' for the important task in hand.

This task fell to John Flamsteed, the first Astronomer Royal, who battled with poor wages and ill health for over 40 years to make over 50,000 observations. His *Historia Coelestis Britannica* was posthumously published in 1725, and without it, the prime meridian would never have ended up at Greenwich.

But the man who finally worked out how to find longitude at sea was a

INSET LEFT
John Flamsteed, the first Astronomer Royal, as seen in a 'Pepper's ghost' image.

LEFT
The Flamsteed Room where the Astronomer Royal received important visitors. Most observations were made in the small quadrant at the bottom of the garden.

Yorkshire-born clock-maker, John Harrison, who worked with Flamsteed's successor, Edmond Halley, to develop a very special and advanced form of sea clock. Regardless of temperature changes at sea his chronometer would always tell the right time.

The problem had been that the position of the sun at any given time varies around the world, so one person's midday need not be another's. The trick was to know your local time from the sun and its difference from the fixed prime meridian; then your longitude could be calculated. A prime meridian had to be set. Where was this to be?

At a conference in Washington in 1884 a majority of delegates from 25 nations decided that the world's prime meridian should be at Greenwich. This was not in deference to the gruelling groundwork done by Flamsteed, but purely pragmatic recognition that by then 72 per cent of world commerce, and most importantly the United States of America, already used Greenwich to set their clocks by.

BELOW
The Time Ball on the observatory roof falls daily at 13.00 hours, and in the days of sail it gave ships on the river a visual time check. On the wall by the gates is the 24-hour clock which has displayed Greenwich time for over a century.

ABOVE
The prime meridian line – longitude zero – runs between the North and South poles. Its position in Greenwich is shown by the line across the observatory courtyard.

· AN INSPIRATION TO DICKENS ·

The first literary mention of London, in AD61, by Tacitus, described it as being crowded with merchants and trading ships. Over many centuries, the momentum did not let up, and by the time the *Téméraire* was broken up in 1838, shipyards were giving way to docks that, together with the wharves and factories, serviced an enormous expansion of trade and industry.

The waterfront had to adapt to the changing times. For example, manufacture of ropes at the Enderby factory site in Greenwich switched to electric cables after the buildings burned down in 1845. The cables produced were later uncoiled over the ocean floors from ships that left here to unleash the first great wave of electronic communication.

Shipbuilding still continued in nearby dockyards – mainly steel barges that joined the motley mixture of wood, iron, steam and sail-powered clippers like the *Cutty Sark* that clogged the river, fetching and carrying goods from around the globe.

Small terraced houses and the pubs that served them proliferated by the river as Greenwich grew into a melting pot of rich and poor. Charles Dickens, a regular of the Trafalgar Tavern, drew inspiration from the urban scene, making its characters famous throughout the world.

LEFT
Visitors have arrived at the present Greenwich Pier since 1836. Pleasure boats operate daily to and from London and to the Thames Barrier by way of the Millennium Dome.

BELOW
Charles Dickens used the Trafalgar Tavern as a background for an episode in Our Mutual Friend. *The tavern was also popular with other famous writers and artists.*

THE CUTTY SARK

The *Cutty Sark*'s great keel was placed on a concrete plinth at Greenwich in 1954. But from the clipper's launch in 1869 until 1895 this keel sliced through the world's oceans at record-breaking speeds, carrying tea from China and later wool from Australia. Even as clippers go, the *Cutty Sark* was always one of the most beautiful, but the coming of steam increasingly took the wind out of her sails and in 1895 she was sold to the Portuguese. The year before she had been seen at full speed by a young Cornish sailor, Wilfred Dowman. He was so inspired by the sight that 28 years later, seeing the *Cutty Sark* in a dilapidated state, he bought and restored her. From 1923 until after the war she became a nautical training ship. If it had not been for the formation of the Cutty Sark Society in the 1950s she would have been broken up and forgotten. Instead she is now a unique reminder of the spectacular age of sail.

BELOW
The ship's figure-head is the bewitched heroine of Robert Burns's poem Tam o'Shanter. She wears a woollen shift or 'cutty sark' and clutches at the horse's tail, as in the legend.

· AN END AND A BEGINNING ·

In the face of growing competition from the north of England and abroad, and disruption during the First World War, Thames trade continued to boom until the depression of 1929. The subsequent slow recovery was then checked by the devastation of the Second World War. In September 1940 German planes tried to bomb the docklands north of the river into oblivion. The Woolwich ferry ran all night evacuating people to south of the river.

But after the war the river traffic revived, and in 1964 wharves and warehouses handled 61 million tons of cargo – a figure never to be exceeded.

Then, with astonishing suddenness, London's life as an international port just vanished. Container shipping and roll-on roll-off ferries made this stretch of the Thames irrelevant. The new container dock 26 miles away at Tilbury had better motorway access, and sucked much of the life out of east London, abandoning the people who had lived and worked there to pick up the pieces. The last London dock closed in 1981.

Most redevelopment so far has taken place across the river from Greenwich on the Isle of Dogs, in Docklands. Here one of London's newest buildings, the 250-metre Canary Wharf Tower, stares across at one of London's oldest, the Greenwich Observatory. Canary Wharf represents a city in which trade is now digital, not water-borne. Dickensian terraced houses, the bijou properties of the beneficiaries of the computer age, stand side by side with estates in which the borough's less fortunate wait hopefully for the jobs to return.

Far Left
Greenwich's rich architectural heritage is complemented by the most daringly innovative new buildings created by modern architects across the river in the Isle of Dogs and Docklands.

Left
Greenwich is a source of interest to many people. Here visitors line the decks of a paddle steamer as it sails upriver.

GIPSY MOTH

THAMES BARRIER
High tide on the Thames is immensely powerful, twice daily sweeping in from the North Sea at 100 metres per minute. A flood in Central London would be devastating; the Thames Barrier was built to prevent it ever happening.
It took ten years to build from 1974 and cost some £500m. The largest of the great retractable gates between the gleaming piers each weigh over 5,000 tons.

Near the *Cutty Sark* is the small but legendary *Gipsy Moth IV*, in which Sir Francis Chichester made the first single-handed voyage around the world in 1966–7, sailing 29,630 miles in 226 days, at the age of 65 and already suffering from cancer. He arrived in Greenwich in July 1967 and was knighted here by Queen Elizabeth II with the same sword which had been used to knight Sir Francis Drake, Elizabeth I's great explorer.

· A GROWING ELEGANCE ·

By the 17th century, Greenwich town was already of considerable size and wealth, and Crooms Hill (one of the oldest roads in London) along the west side of the park had always been one of its most prosperous streets. The Ranger's House (1699) at the top of it is an outstanding redbrick mansion which now houses the Suffolk Collection of eminent old portraits. At around the same time Nicholas Hawksmoor built the imposing Classical church of St Alfege at the bottom of the hill. From here the town centre, including the well-known Arts & Crafts Market, is largely defined by a Regency new town plan designed by Joseph Kay between 1829 and 1843. The famous Trafalgar Tavern (built in 1837) by the river east of the Royal Naval College is one of Kay's creations. Charles Dickens was just one of the 'in crowd' who liked it here. West of the College, where the *Cutty Sark* now stands in its permanent dry dock, the riverside was once a confused sprawl of lanes serving the busy river. East of the Trafalgar Tavern a few things were a touch more grand. One fine

CHARLTON
Charlton, sandwiched between Greenwich and Woolwich, has one of the finest Jacobean mansions in London. Charlton House, built in 1607, remained in private hands until 1925, and is now the capital's most elegantly housed community centre.

BELOW
Vanbrugh is said to have modelled his 'castle' on the Bastille in Paris, where he was once imprisoned.

OPPOSITE ABOVE RIGHT
The Ranger's House (1699) houses an impressive array of Jacobean portraits.

OPPOSITE CENTRE RIGHT
The Museum of Artillery in the Rotunda, Woolwich, houses a unique collection of ordnance and artillery. The Rotunda was once a bell tent erected for the Prince Regent in 1814 in St James's Park. It was moved in 1819 and given a lead roof by John Nash.

early building that still stands is the Trinity Hospital, opened in 1614 and rebuilt in 1812. Further east, towards the Greenwich peninsula, the typically confident home of the 19th-century Enderby family is now the office of the present cable company. Sir John Vanbrugh, who helped design the Greenwich Hospital, built himself Vanbrugh Castle east of Greenwich Park on Maze Hill in 1719. This grim romantic folly was restored in 1977. Up and over the hill on the other side of Blackheath, Sir John Morden, who made his fortune in shipping, in 1695 used an existing estate to found an influential philanthropic charity to house elderly shipping merchants. In the 19th century his Morden College became one of Greenwich's main developers. Many of the small terraced houses built at that time to house the influx of new workers still bear the mark 'MC 1695'.

THE FAN MUSEUM

Housed in two beautifully restored early-Georgian houses on Crooms Hill is the world's only museum devoted to the art and craft of the fan. Besides the permanent collection of this elegant fashion accessory from a bygone age, there are regular changing exhibitions, an orangery and a small Japanese garden.

· MODERN DEVELOPMENTS ·

Greenwich's 20th-century development has both scarred and enhanced the borough. In 1902 the ferry across the Thames from Cutty Sark Gardens to the Isle of Dogs was replaced by the Foot Tunnel, lined with 200,000 tiles. In the same year building began on a new power station – argumentatively close to the ancient Trinity Hospital – which purists appreciate for its interesting mixture of Edwardian 'Church Gothic' and industrial functionalism. The four chimneys should have been higher, but the Astronomer Royal said the smoke would obscure the heavens.

Bombs and town improvements have removed most of the riverside's dark alleys, but not everything that has replaced them has been particularly imaginative. Some pockets of more radical successes remain, like the controversial Span houses which caused a rumpus in old Blackheath when a disciple of Walter Gropius replaced Regency façades with them. The huge dome built on the peninsula to celebrate the new Millennium has proved similarly controversial.

At the beginning of the Millennium much new development is being planned for the area. Ironically, just as historic Greenwich has been designated a World Heritage Site, its significance thus on a par with the Taj Mahal, the borough is also about to become home to one of the biggest concentrations of new buildings in London.

ABOVE LEFT
A picture of elegance. Ornate shapes at the entrance to Greenwich Park from the town.

ABOVE CENTRE
The main guardhouse at the entrance to the Royal Arsenal, Woolwich. The arsenal contains many historic buildings, some of which will form part of a planned heritage centre.

RIGHT
Trinity Hospital was founded as almshouses by the Earl of Northampton in 1614, and his effigy is an imposing feature of the chapel. It gained its crenellated parapets in a 19th-century neo-Gothic restoration. The Mercers' Company select 20 pensioners, who still live here.

ELTHAM

Eltham is home to an astonishing architectural hybrid: the country's most extravagant 1930s house has been grafted onto the remains of a medieval palace. Eltham Palace was first used as a royal residence in 1311, gradually evolving until Tudor Greenwich Palace began to eclipse it. Following the Civil War Eltham slowly decayed, and the magnificent 15th-century Great Hall became a barn, painted by Turner in 1790. In 1933 the millionaire Stephen Courtauld and his wife Virginia were allowed to demolish ruined Victorian additions to build a country house on condition that they restored the Great Hall. Over the next four years they created a sumptuous monument to the Modern Movement with the splendid Hall at one end.

· THE PURSUIT OF PLEASURE ·

The pomp of Greenwich's high architecture conceals an otherwise typically dockside proletarian past, with a big working-class electorate. Gladstone appealed to these people for help in 1868 when he needed a new constituency from which to fight the Tories. After a mass meeting on Blackheath the town adopted him. As the new prime minister, Gladstone and his liberal supporters became regulars at the Trafalgar Tavern's famous whitebait suppers.

The heath has a history of massed rallies in support of radical causes. Another thing that has regularly brought the population out in force is hedonism. Almost as soon as the public were let into Greenwich Park in the 18th century, some of them began to lose control. An early craze was the sometimes dangerous pastime of 'tumbling' (throwing yourself down a hill). Rowdy 'out-of-towners' soon got the bug, and by the 1840s this rough and tumbling had grown into the vast Greenwich Fair which attracted as many as 150,000 people. When it was abolished in 1857 the crowds simply walked up the hill to the Blackheath Fair.

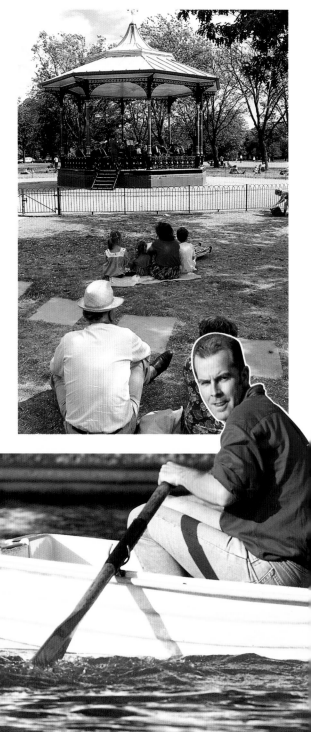

ABOVE RIGHT
Visiting bands often entertain residents and the many Londoners and visitors who come to relax in the oldest of the capital's royal parks.

RIGHT
The boating lake and playground at the foot of Greenwich Park are popular with young children during the summer. An ornamental lake with wild fowl lies on higher ground in the park.

Oxleas Wood, the only survival of south-east London's medieval forests, is a haven for wild life. A deer grazes in the Wilderness in Greenwich Park, a descendant perhaps of the herd introduced by Henry VIII in 1535.

RIGHT
Greenwich Park, with its rolling lawns, ancient Spanish chestnut trees and colourful formal gardens, is a favourite haunt of artists.

BLACKHEATH

Blackheath has often been at the centre of historical events. In 1381 Wat Tyler gathered more than 100,000 people here to protest against the poll tax. In 1415 Henry V returned from Agincourt to be congratulated by 20,000 Londoners on the heath. In 1497 another tax riot, by Cornishmen, led to a pitched battle in which about 1,000 died. In the next century Henry VIII's fourth wife, Anne of Cleves, was greeted here before she was led down to Greenwich Palace. Village life began south-east of the heath in the 1740s, given impetus by the opening of the great Morden College in 1695. Within 50 years an elegant garden suburb had emerged. It still retains its architectural variety and charm.

· A PLACE TO RELAX IN ·

The eminent Greenwich Theatre is on the site of one of the town's 19th-century music halls, which find their modern counterpart nearby in London's most anarchic comedy venue, Up The Creek. The Greenwich and Docklands International Festival brings together these and other venues, such as the Blackheath Concert Halls (the city's oldest), for London's biggest annual arts event every summer. And on the fringes *ad hoc* arts and music collectives with names like Suture and Gold-fish spring up to re-animate abandoned buildings with club nights and installations. At weekends Greenwich is one of the busiest places in London. The combination of sights, shops, famous market, and places to eat and drink, have turned this into one of the country's top tourist destinations. It all speaks of an energy that has gathered momentum with the Millennium, attracting people, ideas and projects to the area like iron filings to a magnet.

LEFT
The opening and closing nights of the annual summer Greenwich and Docklands International Festival end with spectacular fireworks displays – the first on the river in front of the Royal Naval College, the finale in Beresford Square, Woolwich.

ABOVE
Dancers, actors, street performers as well as instrumentalists and singers of classical, jazz and popular music participate in the annual festival.

GREENWICH MARKET

ABOVE AND INSET
Arts and crafts stalls spill out of the covered market in Greenwich at weekends, and specialist dealers set up stalls on Thursdays and Fridays.

LEFT
Greenwich Theatre has attracted stars of stage and screen to perform in classic and modern plays for the last 25 years.

RIGHT
Restaurants abound in Greenwich town centre, offering a huge variety of food. Many pubs not only specialize in food and drink but have lunchtime and evening music.

· THE MILLENNIUM FESTIVITIES ·

The impetus behind the Millennium festivities in Greenwich is not only about celebration. The focus has increasingly moved away from concentration on a point in time towards a commitment to the future. Read the publicity superlatives, and promises threaten to float off the page: the largest dome in the world – more than a kilometre in circumference; 14 themed areas of attractions and exhibits; spectacular live shows daily; 15,000 new jobs; 130 acres of new waterfront development and an economic regeneration that will see new housing, parks and retail outlets. The Jubilee underground line has made its way to Greenwich, and so has the Docklands Light Railway. These are observable facts. And where stray mongrels once roamed on the derelict Greenwich peninsula, a stream of lorries and pile drivers have hammered home the message that more is happening here than has for 50 years. If celebrations in the Millennium Dome relate to the nation as a

ABOVE
A computerised impression of one of the spectacular exhibitions inside the vast millennium dome.